GORSETH KERNOW

The Cornish Gorsedd

what it is and what it does

Rod Lyon

Tewennow

Introduction

From Vanessa Beeman, Gwenenen, Barth Mur

Dynargh dhe'n lyvryk-ma adro dh'agan Gorseth Kernow. Lyes huny re dhervynnas deryvadow yn hy hever, ha pys da on ny y'n tor-ma dh'y dharbary, grassa dhe Rod Lyon, Tewennow, nep a'n scryfas, ha'n para a dhylloryon.

Welcome to this little book about our Cornish Gorsedd. Many people have asked for information about it, and we are pleased now that we can provide it, thanks to Rod Lyon, Tewennow, and the editorial team.

Mys Metheven 2008.

First published in July 2008 by Gorseth Kernow.

Design by Daniel Benney, danielbenney@yahoo.co.uk

Printed by Rowe the Printers, Guildford Road Industrial Estate, Hayle, Cornwall TR27 4PZ.

ISBN: 978-1-903668-04-7

Front Cover Picture: Gorseth Kernow at Predannack, Mullion, 1957. Ann Trevenen Jenkin. Back Cover: J. Chesterfield initiates Jory Ansell as Grand Bard, Roche Rock, 1991.

Contents

What is a Gorsedd and how did it all start?

1

Gorsedd means in English 'a Bardic Assembly', and comes from the ancient Celtic word *uerensed*, meaning 'high seat' or 'throne'.

Bard derives from the name given by Greek writers to the poets and musicians associated with priests and Druids — *bardoi*.

Originally the term *bard* was generally conferred upon all professional poets. It would seem that in Britain (and Ireland), there were official bards attached to each court. In the early British courts, the bard's most important function was that of custodian of the genealogies. Bards therefore were very prestigious persons and often the closest personal ties existed between them and their patrons.

The most important bard in the court was the 'chief of song' – the *Penkerd* – followed by the 'Bard of the royal entourage' – the *Bard Teylu*. According to Welsh Laws, the former had his land free, and sat next to the appointed heir in the hall, his function being to sing to the prince. The *Bard Teylu* also had his land free, and his horse from the prince, as well as his harp and a gold ring from his queen. He sang second to the *Penkerd*, and his seat in the hall was lower.

Head of all the bards in the Gorsedd was, and still is, The Grand Bard. He was eleventh in order of precedence at the royal court and on his installation he was presented with gifts from the prince and his queen. Being Grand Bard, he was head of all the Bardic Order, and his symbol of authority was the great chair in which he sat.

Taliesin

Although there had been bards in Britain certainly as early as the time of the Romans, the founding of the Bardic Order has been attributed to Taliesin, who lived in the 6th century. His poetry is among the oldest remaining bardic works. He, like other bards, travelled from court to court singing and reciting his epic tales, and it is through this that we have gleaned much of early Celtic life and history.

Boscawen Un

The *Gorseddau* or 'Bardic Assemblies', where bards met for their ceremonies and contests for music, singing and literature, took place across Britain, and one of the three chief places was at 'Beisgawen' in 'Dyfnwal'. 'Dyfnwal' was what we recognise today as Dumnonia – or Cornwall and Devon, and 'Beisgawen' has been identified with Boscawen Un, in the parish of St Buryan, west of Penzance. Stone circles, however, such as that at Boscawen Un, have been dated to about 2,000 BC, long before the Celts settled in Britain, but it is thought that their very important and hallowed status made them appropriate sites for the early gorseddau.

Unfortunately there are no records of any early Cornish bards, probably due to the elimination of the Cornish kingdoms by the Saxons, and therefore of the bards who were part of them.

Iolo Morganwg

The bardic tradition in Wales also grew very weak, but a thread of continuity did prevail, and with the revival of interest in early British history in the 18th century, a revived Gorsedd in Wales was held in the year 1792. This was devised by Edward Williams or Iolo Morganwg (Iolo of Glamorgan) and followed a definite code of rules and ceremonies. Although initially criticised, the Welsh Gorsedd continued, and in 1819 it was combined for the first time with one of the Welsh *eisteddfodau*, these having been held continuously in Wales since 1177. This now gave to the Welsh Gorsedd a permanent anchor.

© 'Steve Hartgroves, Historic Environment Service, Cornwall County Council

© Steve Hartgroves

THE CORNISH GORSEDD

above Boscawen Un
right Iolo Morganwg

How did this affect Cornwall and the introduction of her Gorsedd?

2

The Cornish Language

The Cornish language may be considered as the main catalyst here. Around the time that Iolo Morganwg devised the 'new' Gorsedd in Wales, the last of the true 'first-language' speakers of Cornish were dying. By 1800, the bulk of Cornish speaking as the vernacular was confined to an ever-decreasing core of people in the Penwith area, and although there is proof that the language continued in a very broken-down and fitful state right through the 19th century, it had lost its true sense of purpose.

However, in 1877 the then vicar of the parish of Paul, the Rev W S Lach-Szyrma, held a celebration to commemorate the 100th anniversary of the death of Dolly Pentreath, a 'fish jowster' of Mousehole in that parish, who became famous for being (incorrectly) identified as the last Cornish speaker. Following this celebration, a renewed desire among a dedicated band of Cornish people was kindled, and work started to get the language off its death-bed and living again.

Henry Jenner

One of these dedicated workers was Henry Jenner. Strangely, at the 1877 Dolly Pentreath celebrations, he was of the same opinion as many other learned individuals of the time – Cornish as a living language was lost and was there only to be studied as a historical exercise. What changed Jenner's attitude towards the language and the Cornish identity generally over the next twenty-five years is not known; it may have been his contacts with Wales and Brittany which were behind the changes, but whatever it was, it was something very influential, because in 1903 he was made a bard of the Breton Gorsedd, taking the bardic name *Gwaz Mikael* – 'The Servant of Michael'. A marked change indeed!

This was followed in 1904 by the publication of his *Handbook of the Cornish Language* – the first really serious attempt at teaching Cornish to 'non-scholarly' people. Also at that year's Celtic Congress in Caernarfon, along with L C R Duncombe Jewell and Joseph Hambley Rowe, he convinced the delegates that

Cornwall and the Cornish were truly Celtic, and in so doing gained Cornwall's recognition as one of the six Celtic Nations.

This latter achievement must have sown the seed in Jenner's mind of a Cornish Gorsedd, because there is a record of him only three years later, in 1907, translating into Cornish parts of the Welsh Gorsedd, 'just in case it might be needed sometime'.

Ten years later, in 1917, Jenner was at Neath for the Welsh Gorsedd, and it was probably here that the initial plans for a Cornish Gorsedd were formulated. At Neath Jenner met D Rhys Phillips (*Beili Glas*), a man who had so much to do ten years later with the setting up of our Gorsedd here in Cornwall.

Old Cornwall Societies

Another catalyst, which was instrumental in getting a Cornish Gorsedd off the ground, was the formation of the Old Cornwall Societies.

The growing sense of Cornish patriotism following the 1877 Dolly Pentreath event led to the first Old Cornwall Society being formed at St Ives in 1920. Thereafter, interest in all things Cornish rapidly increased, and in no time Old Cornwall societies were springing up all over Cornwall; within four years there were sufficient societies to form what became and what still is the Federation of Old Cornwall Societies.

It would appear from the events which followed that a Cornish Gorsedd was now a certainty. In 1927 Jenner, dressed in his Breton bardic robes and head-dress, attended a meeting at

left Trethevy, St Cleer (1952)

Boscawen Un, where he read a paper discussing the significance of the stone circle there in Taliesin's time and the bardic link down to Iolo Morganwg's setting up of the new Welsh Gorsedd in 1792. Furthermore, as this was one of the three main sites of the Gorseddau of Ancient Britain, it would, he felt, be an ideal setting for any Cornish Gorsedd.

Robert Morton Nance

Jenner, however, was now getting old – he was 79 in 1927 – and so the cause was taken up by another Cornish stalwart – Robert Morton Nance. It was following a visit that year by Nance to the first post-war Breton Gorsedd, where he had a meeting with D Rhys Phillips, that it became quite clear that plans to set up a Cornish Gorsedd were well advanced. Letters passed with some frequency between the two, and Phillips who had, virtually on his own initiative, set in motion the mechanism by which a Cornish Gorsedd could be founded, had advanced so far that he suggested the Duchy should invite 'a group of Chief Gorsedd officials, who would emblazon the history of Cornwall by carrying out a Gorsedd celebration such as never was on land or sea.' He even got to the point of suggesting that Jenner should be the first Grand Bard, that Nance should be his deputy, and that he (Nance) should organise, with Jenner, the complete ceremony to suit Cornwall and that he (Phillips) would 'legalise' it.

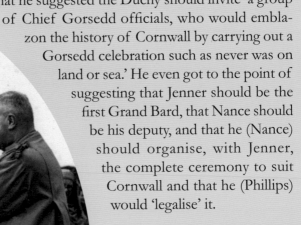

12

Federation of Old Cornwall Societies

The recently-formed Federation of Old Cornwall Societies now therefore became involved and at its conference in February 1928, it was agreed that the officials of the Welsh Gorsedd be invited to hold a ceremony in Cornwall, with a view to forming a Cornish Gorsedd. A formal petition was drawn up and sent to the Welsh Gorsedd of Bards requesting them to hold a gorsedd at Boscawen Un during the month of September and, 'if it so pleases you, then and there to inaugurate a Cornish Gorsedd and to confer on it such sanction and powers as are necessary for its validity.' The petition was signed by Jenner, Nance and Alfred Kenneth Hamilton Jenkin, as President, Recorder and Honorary Secretary, respectively, of the Federation.

Treorchy, 1928

The Welsh Gorsedd, following a Proclamation Ceremony held in June 1928 at Liverpool, was in favour, and it was recommended that ten worthy Cornish people be initiated at the next Welsh Gorsedd at Treorchy in August in readiness as the core of the new Cornish Gorsedd.

The original ten names were eventually reduced to eight. Likewise the original recommendation that the members of the proposed Cornish Gorsedd should be, as in Wales, dressed in white, blue or green, according to each individual's station, did not go ahead. Nance persuaded Phillips that in Cornwall it was the desire that *all* members of the Gorsedd should be treated equally and wear the blue of bards, beause it was impossible to distinguish their merits. This was reluctantly agreed to, and since its inception, the Cornish Gorsedd has maintained the 'one-colour' stance, the only distinguishing feature being that senior bards and holders of office have a different style of head-dress or wear plastrons (ceremonial breastplates).

right Boscawen Un (1928)

Druids, ovates and bards

This single colour system which operates in Cornwall means that there are no such positions within the Gorsedd as Druids (dressed in white) or Ovates (dressed in green). A further difference in Cornwall is that the leader is styled 'Grand Bard' and not 'Archdruid' as in Wales, or 'Grand Druid' as in Brittany.

Following their admission at Treorchy, seven of the eight Cornish bards met in the long-demolished *Cox's Café* in Cardiff, and constituted themselves, together with Jenner and his wife, as the Council of *Gorseth Kernow* (The Cornish Gorsedd). As suggested earlier by Phillips, it was decided that Jenner should be Grand Bard and Nance his deputy. This newly formed Council confirmed in addition that members of the Cornish Gorsedd should be in only one degree, that of bard, 'until the Council shall determine otherwise', and that the rules for 'the Governance of the Gorsedd be decided by the Council at a later meeting.' Also discussed were the appropriate qualifications for bardship and agreement on a number of other Cornish men and women to be initiated at the forthcoming Gorsedd at Boscawen Un. A particular requirement agreed at the meeting, and one which is still a prerequisite today, was that any candidate for admission into the Gorsedd should 'exhibit a manifestation of the Celtic spirit.'

The first Gorsedd and the early days

3

Boscawen Un, 1928

Everything was ready and in place by the last ten days of September, 1928, and following extensive coverage in the *Western Morning News*, the first *Gorseth Kernow* was inaugurated at Boscawen Un on the 21st of the month.

Having lunched and robed at St Buryan, Archdruid *Pedrog* of Wales, accompanied by Deputy Archdruid *Elfed* and ten other members of the Gorsedd of Bards

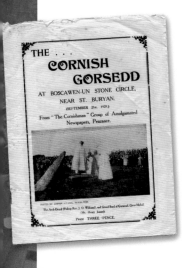

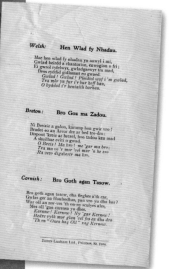

of Wales, joined the eight Cornish bards admitted in August at Treorchy, together with a dozen bare-headed initiates, members of the Old Cornwall Societies and the mayors of seven Cornish boroughs. Led by Penzance Silver Band, they all processed from Boscawen Farm to the circle.

Following the call to the four corners of Cornwall by *Corn Gwlas* (the Horn of the Nation) and the singing of the Gorsedd Prayer, the ceremony was opened by Archdruid *Pedrog*. He received the Fruits of the Earth from the Lady of Cornwall, and 'proclaimed the Cornish Gorsedd and gave his benison to it'. Henry Jenner was installed as Grand Bard, before in turn admitting the twelve initiates as bards and announcing that there would be another Gorsedd, the details of which were to be considered. The ceremony, which was conducted in Cornish, Welsh and English, was brought to an end with the singing of *Bro Goth Agan Tasow* – Old Land of Our Fathers.

Following the ceremony, there was a civic reception in St John's Hall, Penzance, this being followed by a meeting of Jenner, Nance and twelve bards, who then appointed an Executive Committee, or Council, with the particular duty of arranging the following year's Gorsedd.

left An early Gorsedd (Carwynnen, 1948)

This Council met the following April, when Carn Brea was chosen as the next site for September of that year. The following year, 1930, the Gorsedd was held at the Hurlers, near St Cleer, since, as was correctly pointed out, 'the Tamar is the boundary of Cornwall, not the Fal'. This plan of moving the site of the Gorsedd around Cornwall has been followed up to the present day, principally with the idea of a west, then central, then east location.

The first Gorsedd (Boscawen Un, 1928)

Language Bards

The basic rules discussed prior to the first Gorsedd at Boscawen Un and set out and agreed in 1929 still apply today, but with the passing of time there have naturally been changes. The admission of 'Bards of Honour' from other countries was introduced in 1930, and two years later the admission of bards via the medium of the Cornish language was allowed.

The first 'Language Bards' all did stalwart work on behalf of the language in those early days, but generally the level of proficiency required in 1932 was basic compared to the high standards of today.

Bardic robes

At this time, the bardic robes took on their current appearance, with the introduction of the black-gold-black bands across the front of the head-dress of ordinary bards and the distinctive head-dress for the Grand Bard, his deputy and later, past Grand Bards. The dress for the Lady of Cornwall also received much consideration, resulting in the design and colour as seen today. Another step forward was the expansion and standardizing of the ceremony, which, with a few basic modifications and further additions, is that which is carried out today.

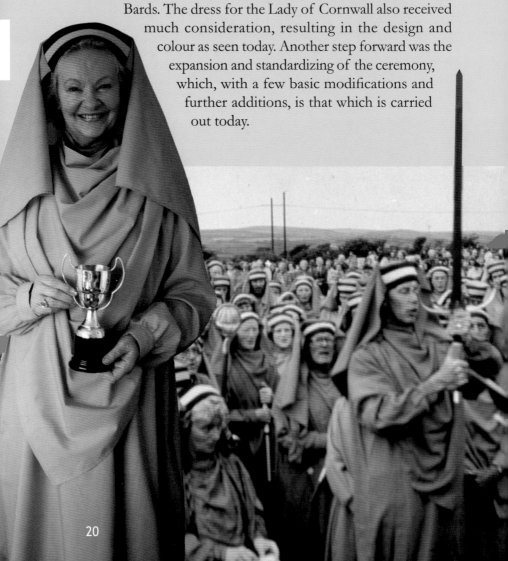

Symbolism

At this point the meaning of one feature common to all three Gorseddau should be explained. This is the display on various items of bardic dress and regalia of the symbol **/ | **, known as the *awen*. *Awen* means 'muse' or 'inspiration' and represents the creative powers in action. It is also known in Welsh as *Y Nod Cyfrin* – 'The Mystic Mark' and *Y Nod Peldyr Goleuni* – 'The Mark of the Shaft of Light', where it is derived from the rays of the rising sun on the longest day – Midsummer – (north of east); the shortest day – Midwinter – (south of east); and the equinox (due east). In the Bardic Gorsedd it is also said to represent the attributes of 'love', 'justice' and 'truth'.

The *awen* symbol of the Cornish Gorsedd appears on the Grand Bard's crown, the head-dress of the Deputy Grand Bard and past Grand Bards, as well as on all the plastrons worn by Grand

and Deputy Grand Bards (past and present) and certain senior officers. It also appears on headed Gorsedd notepaper.

In May 1934, Henry Jenner, the first Grand Bard, who had been instrumental in setting up a Cornish Gorsedd, died at the age of 85. The automatic choice for a new Grand Bard was Robert Morton Nance.

Nance was duly installed in 1934 and was to continue as Grand Bard until his death in 1959. With the passing of Nance, the period of tenure was changed to a maximum of three years, with an optional further three years if so approved by the Gorsedd Council.

A wider role

With Nance at the helm, the Gorsedd became more outward-looking, not just restricting its activities to within the bardic circle. At this time, in the mid-1930s, there were a number of bards – and members of the public – who considered that the Gorsedd was still too inward-looking, and although by 1936 there were around 140 bards, it was felt that not enough was being done to fulfil the obligations of the 'Manifestation of the Celtic Spirit.'

Meetings therefore took place with the Cornwall Music Festival and the Cornwall Education Authority, following which a much broader field of competitions was introduced, paving the way for the diverse selection we have today. Enthusiasm among younger Cornish people was strong and in the first year of literary awards in 1937, no fewer than 107 essays were submitted.

opposite, clockwise from top Gorsedd concert (St Just 1998)
Jory Ansell at the grave of Henry Jenner (1994)
The bilingual sign on Tamar bridge, unveiled 2008

Welcome to
CORNWALL
KERNOW
a'gas dynergh

The present and the future

4

Who can become a bard?

Slowly but surely, too, people from different walks of life in Cornwall were invited to join the Gorsedd. Today, of course, people may be nominated for bardship and accepted within the Gorsedd for any one of a whole range of activities. In addition to literature, music, language and the arts generally, there are sports personalities, people who have worked assiduously for Cornwall in social, economic and even leisure activities, and those who have maintained within their own communities a recognition and awareness of their Cornish identity. Today, it does not matter in what field a

24

particular person's interest might lie, nor does he or she have to be Cornish or live in Cornwall, as long as that particular person's activity is beneficial to Cornwall, her people, culture, heritage and identity.

Since its inception, over 1,150 bards have been created, of which more than half are still alive. Not all are Cornish, and not all are resident in Cornwall. There are bards in Australia and North America, invited to become bards because of their work in promoting Cornwall and Cornishness to the emigrant families in those countries, and many of these make the long trip to Cornwall – often more than once – to be initiated into the Gorsedd and attend the Gorsedd ceremonies.

How does one become a bard?

A person who is considered worthy of bardship must be proposed and seconded by two existing bards, who are required to submit independent citations to the Gorsedd in support of their candidate. These citations must be presented without the knowledge of the person being nominated. Each nominee is in turn considered by the Gorsedd Council based on the citations received, and if found satisfactory, is duly invited to become a bard. Bards accepting the invitation choose a Bardic Name, in Cornish, which is generally either relevant to their place of birth, their particular vocation, or the work which has led them to be invited into the Gorsedd. This name is entirely of their own choosing, but it has to be one not previously used, cannot thereafter be changed, and must be approved by the Grand Bard.

The names of these new bards are not made public until ten days before their official acceptance into the Gorsedd, now always held on the first Saturday in September.

GRAND BARD
John Bolitho

28

Grand Bard and Deputy Grand Bard

Grand Bards and Deputy Grand Bards can be men or women, the first female Grand Bard being chosen in 1997. Both are elected for a maximum of three years by the Gorsedd Council which, chaired by the Grand Bard, meets regularly throughout the year to monitor and decide on Gorsedd policy and to authorize the appointment of new bards.

l-r Past Grand Bard, John Bolitho
Former Deputy Grand Bard, E E Morton Nance **29**

The Open Gorsedd

The colourful ceremony witnessed at the Open Gorsedd is one of only two public meetings of all bards in their robes. The other occasion on which robes are worn is the Proclamation Gorsedd ceremony, which now takes place on the third Saturday in April and, as the name suggests, 'proclaims' the date of that year's Open Gorsedd and is held at its site. The ceremony is much shorter than the Gorsedd itself. Bardic robes are also worn when the Celtic Congress returns to Cornwall every six years and *may* be worn by individuals on other special occasions, but only with the express approval of the Grand Bard or the Council. The Grand and Deputy Grand Bards wear special plastrons when representing the Gorsedd at civic functions.

The ceremony of the Open Gorsedd – where bards are 'on view' to the public – has been held annually since 1928, though during the war years a scaled-down version was used, at Nance's house in Carbis Bay in 1939 and at the Royal Institution of Cornwall in Truro from 1940 to 1945.

Challenging times

Apart from slow and steady modifications over the years, the Gorsedd has changed very little. However, with the considerably larger number of bards now attending each annual Gorsedd ceremony, and the correspondingly increased facilities required for their accommodation, the organisation of the day has become much more complicated.

From the early days, much of this organisation has been undertaken by the particular Old Cornwall Society in whose area the Gorsedd has been held. This was not too strenuous a task when

right Trencrom 1953. The 25th Year

fewer than a hundred bards attended, but catering for upwards of three hundred is getting beyond the capabilities of all but the most conscientious and energetic Society.

In addition, finding both a hall where this number can enjoy the traditional Bardic Tea after the Gorsedd ceremony and an indoor venue for the ceremony itself in the event of rain is becoming increasingly difficult. Although we have been blessed with dry weather on all but a handful of occasions during the Gorsedd's existence, the shortened version that the public witnesses when it does rain lacks atmosphere, the main casualty being the traditional circle of bards.

Although the original plan was to select a Gorsedd site with some historic significance, it is now more usual, largely because of the growing number of bards, to choose a school sports field for the ceremony and to use the school building itself for robing and the Bardic Tea.

The Gorsedd year

The work to safeguard the integrity of Cornwall against cultural, political and economic threats continues throughout the year. The high profile that Gorseth Kernow enjoys is recognized in both the Council of Europe and the European Parliament. The Grand Bard, his or her deputy and many other bards are actively involved in such events as St Piran's Day (March 5th), Esethvos Kernow (The Cornish Eisteddfod, which is held annually in the run-up

right Bardic initiates (Perran Round, 1992)

to the Gorsedd), Dehwelans, the major Cornish homecoming festival which takes place every two or three years, the Celtic Congress and the Royal Cornwall Show. An annual Conference Day is also a feature of the Gorsedd calendar.

clockwise from top left Bards gather in
Canada, Australia and America.

THE CORNISH GORSEDD

Beyond the Tamar, Gorseth Kernow supports the activities of
the various Cornish associations in England and Wales, awarding
the Paul Smales Medallion for services to Cornwall by someone living outside Cornwall. A number of Cornish associations
for exiles also sponsor awards. Individual bards attend the St
David's Day Parade in Cardiff on March 1st, and the Gorsedd
is usually represented at both Eisteddfod Genedlaethol Cymru
(The Welsh National Eisteddfod) and the Breton Gorsedd.

Less public, but just as important, is the work of the various
committees in such fields as the Cornish language, archives and
publications, competitions and awards.

Although it does not promote any particular spelling system,
the Gorsedd strongly supports the use and development of
Kernewek (the Cornish language) and in 2007 the Council
agreed a submission to the Commission on a Standard Written
Form of Cornish which urged prompt action and minimum
disruption. The Standard Written Form has now been finalised,
and it is likely that the Gorseth Council will recommend for
approval its use for official purposes.

Of the numerous annual awards, one of the most labour-inten-
sive is the Holyer an Gof Trophy for prestigious publications
on Cornwall or Cornish themes, which involves a committee
of bards reading and judging between sixty and seventy books
published during the previous calendar year.

Although Gorseth Kernow is neither political nor affiliated
to any religion, many bards are politically active in the more
Cornwall-centred parties and organisations which campaign
for devolved powers for Cornwall, while others are involved
in organising the church services in Cornish held on special
occasions throughout the year.

The Cornish Diaspora

The Gorsedd has a long tradition of supporting people of Cornish descent around the world, many of whom, in turn, submit entries in its competitions. Indeed, it is rare that someone from the diaspora is not honoured at the annual Gorsedd ceremony, with either bardship or an award.

The Grand Bard (sometimes accompanied by other bards) invariably attends Kernewek Lowender, 'the world's largest Cornish festival', on the Yorke Peninsula, South Australia. Other assemblies and ceremonies of Cornish bards in Canada and the United States are supported by Gorseth Kernow.

The future

In establishing Gorseth Kernow, Henry Jenner and Robert Morton Nance held out the prospect of Cornwall as a cultural land in its own right, with Kernewek at its heart. That prospect is now closer than ever.

In 2002 Cornish was recognized by central government as one of Britain's official regional or minority languages, and shortly afterwards central funding for Cornish-language projects became available. Bards of Gorseth Kernow were active in the process to establish a Standard Written Form of the language for official and public use, thus building on the pioneering work done by earlier bards.

Over the years Gorseth Kernow has been at the forefront of the campaign for a Cornish university. It is, therefore, encouraging that, at its Cornwall Campus at Tremough, the University of Exeter now offers first-degree courses in subjects such as 'History and Cornish Studies' and 'Politics and Cornish Studies', as well as further degrees in 'Cornish Studies'.

All the signs are, then, that Gorseth Kernow will continue to uphold the national Celtic spirit of Cornwall, defend her integrity and promote her distinctiveness.

left A tripartite Gorsedd in Brittany, 1999, to commemorate 100 years of the Breton Gorsedd. The plates which show the emblems of the three countries were made by Henriot Pottery, Brittany, to mark the occasion. Pictured are the three leaders of (l-r) Cornwall, Brittany and Wales.

The Gorsedd ceremony

5

Many who have attended the Gorsedd ceremony are unaware of its significance, and therefore a brief description of each part is given to enable the viewing public to fully understand its history and meaning. Much of it is based on the Welsh Gorsedd and has changed very little over the years.

The parts of the ceremony requiring explanation are as follows.

The ceremony begins with the sounding of **Corn Gwlas** (The Horn of the Nation) to the four points of the compass, a symbolic call to all Cornwall.

Garm Cres (The Cry of Peace) is performed by the Grand Bard, who thrice cries, **"Us Cres?"** (Is there Peace?) On the bards replying **"Cres!"** (Peace!), the Gorsedd is declared open by him or her.

Offryn Frutys an Nor (The Offering of the Fruits of the Earth), symbolic of God's gifts to mankind, is performed by a lady who acts on behalf of the women and children of Cornwall.

Arta ef a Dhe (He shall come again) refers to the old belief that Arthur is to return and restore the nationhood of Cornwall. He is accepted by the bards as symbolising the Celtic Spirit.

Cofheans Ysyly us Tremenys (The Commemoration of Deceased Bards) is the announcement of the names of those bards who have died since the previous Gorsedd.

Degemeryans Byrth Noweth (Initiation of New Bards) appropriately follows the above commemoration, symbolically showing that the work of the Gorsedd is being carried on.

Arethyow Cot (Short Speeches). These are greetings brought to Gorseth Kernow by delegates from the Gorseddau of Wales and Brittany.

Ryansow an Orseth (Gorsedd Awards) are prizes presented to the winners of competitions, and awards for particular services rendered to Cornwall.

Cledha Myghtern Arthur (The Sword of King Arthur) is the swearing of allegiance to Cornwall as a Celtic Nation on this symbolic weapon. Bards unable to reach the sword itself lay a hand on the shoulder of one in contact with it.

Bro Goth Agan Tasow (Old Land of our Fathers) is the Cornish version of the Welsh Hen Wlad fy Nhadau, which was adopted as the Celtic Anthem at the Celtic Congress at Caernarfon in 1904.

Garm Cres (The Cry of Peace) is repeated and the Gorsedd pronounced closed.

right Robert Morton Nance initiates Claude Berry (Boscawen Un,1950)

Explanatory notes

6

Spectators at the Gorsedd may not recognise or realise the significance of many of the items of regalia worn by bards or used during the ceremony, and so the following notes and photographs are provided by way of explanation.

above A.B. Venning, with Grand Bard, Gunwyn (1969)

The Grand Bard's Crown

The First Grand Bard, Henry Jenner, did not wear a crown, but decorated his Breton head-dress with a circlet of ivy and mistletoe. When Nance became Grand Bard on the death of Jenner in 1934, he designed and fashioned his own small copper chaplet of laurel leaves which, due to its deteriorating condition, was replaced in 1966 by a similarly designed copper crown. At about the same time another copper crown of oak leaves was commissioned. This is the crown now worn by the Grand Bard during the ceremony, while the crown of laurel leaves is used at the installation every three years of a new Grand Bard. Both crowns bear the *awen* symbol and the copper for each – as is the case for all of the regalia of the Gorsedd – should be Cornish.

The Grand Bard's Principal Crown is worn throughout the Gorsedd ceremony and whenever he or she attends gorseddau outside Cornwall

The Grand Bard's Second Crown is worn every three years by the retiring Grand Bard on the installation of his or her successor.

left E.G Retallack Hooper (Talek), Grand Bard, at Camborne (1960)   43

The Bardic Chair

The bardic chair, used by the Grand Bard at the Open Gorsedd ceremony, was designed, made and donated by bard Les Libby *(Pengover)* in 1982. The cushion was designed, fabricated and donated by the Cornish Guild of Spinners, Weavers and Dyers in 1990. When not in use, the chair is on public display in Truro Cathedral.

Bards' Head-dress

This is blue, but in place of the black headband and *awen* of the Deputy Grand Bard's head-dress, it has three horizontal bands, black-yellow-black. The three bands were introduced in 1932, before which the entire head-dress was blue.

Past Grand Bards' Head-dress

This is yellow with a black headband, emblazoned, like that of
the Deputy Grand Bard, with a yellow *awen*. The headband itself,
however, is higher and shaped differently. The specific head-
dress of a Past Grand Bard was introduced in the 1960s.

The Grand Bard's Plastron

This is the ceremonial breastplate, worn
at all the public ceremonies. It is of
beaten copper, and displays not only the
awen symbol, but also the fifteen bezants of
the Shield of Cornwall. It was made by Francis
Cargeeg (*Tan Dyvarow*) of Hayle.

List of Grand Bards and their years of office

7

Name	Bardic Name	Years in office
Henry Jenner	Gwas Myghal	1928 – 1934
R Morton Nance	Mordon	1934 – 1959
E G R Hooper	Talek	1959 – 1964
G Pawley White	Gunwyn	1964 – 1970
D A Trevanion	Trevanyon	1970 – 1976
Richard Jenkin	Map Dyvroeth	1976 – 1982
Hugh Miners	Den Toll	1982 – 1985
Richard Jenkin	Map Dyvroeth	1985 – 1988
John Chesterfield	Gwas Costentyn	1988 – 1991
George Ansell	Caradok	1991 – 1994
Rev. Brian Coombes	Cummow	1994 – 1997
Ann Trevenen Jenkin	Bryallen	1997 – 2000
John Bolitho	Jowan an Cleth	2000 – 2003
Rod Lyon	Tewennow	2003 – 2006
Vanessa Beeman	Gwenenen	2006 -

List of Deputy Grand Bards and their years of office

8

Name	Bardic Name	Years in office
R Morton Nance	Mordon	1928 – 1934
J Hambley Rowe	Tolzethan	1934 – 1937
Trelawny Roberts	Gonader A-bell	1937 – 1946
Henry Trefusis	Map Mor	1946 – 1952
Rev. D R Evans	Gwas Cadoc	1952 – 1962
F B Cargeeg	Tan Dyvarow	1962 – 1967
Maj. C H Beer	Map Kenwyn	1967 – 1972
Richard Jenkin	Map Dyvroeth	1972 – 1976
Hugh Miners	Den Toll	1976 – 1982
E E Morton Nance	Gwas Gwethnok	1982 – 1988
George Ansell	Caradok	1988 – 1991
Rev. Brian Coombes	Cummow	1991 – 1994
Ann Trevenen Jenkin	Bryallen	1994 – 1997
John Bolitho	Jowan an Cleth	1997 – 2000
Rod Lyon	Tewennow	2000 – 2003
Vanessa Beeman	Gwenenen	2003 - 2006
Mick Paynter	Skogynn Pryv	2006 -

left Gorseth Proclamation, St Keverne, at the start of the Keskerdh
Kernow Walk to London, May 1997. Rev. Brian Coombes (Cummow)
Grand Bard

List of Gorsedd sites

9

1928	Boscawen Un
1929	Carn Brea
1930	The Hurlers, St Cleer
1931	Penzance
1932	Merry Maidens, St Buryan
1933	Roche Rock
1934	Padderbury Top, Menheniot
1935	Penzance
1936	Kelly Round, Wadebridge
1937	Boscawen Un
1938	Trippet Stones, Bodmin
1939	'Chylason', Carbis Bay
1940	RIC Truro
1941	RIC Truro
1942	RIC Truro
1943	RIC Truro
1944	RIC Truro
1945	RIC Truro
1946	Perran Round, Goonhavern
1947	Launceston
1948	Carwynnen, Camborne
1949	Mount Charles Menhyr
1950	Boscawen Un
1951	Padstow
1952	Trethevy, St Cleer
1953	Trencrom, Lelant
1954	Castle Dore, Golant
1955	Merry Maidens, St Buryan

left Gorseth Proclamation, Truro. 1989

1956	Castle Canyke, Bodmin
1957	Predannack, Mullion
1958	Perran Round, Goonhavern
1959	Callington
1960	Camborne
1961	Bude Castle
1962	Barrowfields, Newquay
1963	Giant's Rock, Zennor
1964	Tintagel
1965	Goodern, Kea
1966	St Ives
1967	Saltash
1968	St Just
1969	Liskeard
1970	Perran Round, Goonhavern
1971	Merry Maidens, St Buryan
1972	Launceston Castle
1973	Mount Charles Menhyr
1974	Glasney, Penryn
1975	Bude Castle
1976	Hayle
1977	Nine Maidens, St Columb Major
1978	Merry Maidens, St Buryan
1979	Bodmin and Boscawen Un (Commemorative Gorsedd)
1980	Saltash
1981	Nance, Illogan
1982	St Just

1983	St Kew
1984	Callington
1985	Perran Round, Goonhavern
1986	Merry Maidens, St Buryan
1987	Antony House
1988	Poldhu, Mullion
1989	Lostwithiel
1990	Marazion
1991	Roche Rock
1992	Perran Round, Goonhavern
1993	Bude Castle
1994	Camborne
1995	Marazion
1996	Liskeard
1997	Bodmin
1998	St Just
1999	Hayle
2000	Falmouth
2001	St Columb
2002	Pensilva
2003	Launceston
2004	Truro
2005	Wadebridge
2006	Redruth
2007	Penzance
2008	Looe

Further information

10

Publications

Gorseth Kernow has either published or sponsored the publication of the following:

Den Toll (Hugh Miners), *Gorseth Kernow: the first 50 years,* Gorseth Kernow, 1978

William Morris (*Haldreyn*), *The Gorsedd and its Bards in Britain,* Gorseth Kernow, reprinted 1988

Garry Tregidga and Treve Crago, *Map Kenwyn: the Life and Times of Cecil Beer,* Gorseth Kernow, 2000

Hugh Miners and Treve Crago, *Tolzethan: the Life and Times of Joseph Hambley Rowe,* Gorseth Kernow, 2002

Derek R Williams (ed), *Henry and Katharine Jenner: A Celebration of Cornwall's Culture, Language and Identity,* Francis Boutle, 2004

Peter W Thomas and Derek R Williams (eds), *Setting Cornwall on its Feet: Robert Morton Nance, 1873-1959,* Francis Boutle, 2007

John Chirgwin Jenkin (comp), *Byrth Gorseth Kernow/Bards of the Gorseth of Cornwall, 1928-2007,* Gorseth Kernow, 2007

Website

The website of Gorseth Kernow, **www.gorsethkernow.org.uk** provides full information about the organisation's history (including film clips of previous gorseddau), ceremonies, activities and publications, as well as contact details for the various office-holders.

Gorseth Administrator: Colin Roberts.
Email: colin.roberts59@btinternet.com Tel: 01637-833430

Acknowledgements

Thanks to:

Members of the Gorseth Publications committee for steering through the project with the author - Terry Knight, Ann Trevenen Jenkin, Peter Thomas and Derek Williams.

Our patient and gifted designer, Daniel Benney of St Agnes, for his expertise and ready help at all times.

For photographs - Gorseth Archives, Gorseth website (Ted Chapman and Susan Davey), Helen Banks (former Gorseth webmaster), MAGA, Cornish World (Nigel Pengelly), Cornwall & Isles of Scilly Press (Phil Monckton), Historic Environment Service, Cornwall County Council, Tim Hosking Photographic, Australia, Ian Dunn, Simon Parker (Western Morning News), David Roberts, Francis Trewin, Steve Hartgroves, Frank Ruhrmund, Terry Knight, Vivian Pryor, Ann Trevenen Jenkin, John Rapson.

Every effort has been made to contact the copyright holders of the photographs used, and we apologise for any omissions.

© Published by Gorseth Kernow, July 2008.

left The Gorseth harpist, Esme Francis

Saltash 1967